Love Burning Deep

Also by Kathy Galloway and published by SPCK:
Imagining the Gospels (1988)

Love Burning Deep

Poems and Lyrics

KATHY GALLOWAY

First published in Great Britain 1993
Society for Promoting Christian Knowledge
Holy Trinity Church
Marylebone Road
London NW1 4DU

British Library Cataloguing-in-Publication Data

A catalogue record for this book is available from the British Library

ISBN 0-281-04642-5

Typeset by Pioneer Associates, Perthshire
Printed in Great Britain by
The Longdunn Press, Bristol

For Ian
fellow traveller

Contents

CONTENTS

CONTENTS

Abbreviations

CH3   *The Church Hymnary*, 3rd edn, Oxford University Press 1988.

SGP   *Songs of God's People*, Oxford University Press 1988.

Preface

*'You can't get out of touch with God every moment that
you live, for the simple reason that God is life: not religious
life nor church life, but the whole life that we now live
in the flesh.'* (George MacLeod)

These writings, poems and lyrics, are the markers of a
seven-year (and still counting) spiritual journey which has
encompassed Iona and Glasgow, Russia and Japan, Mauritius
and Israel and the Occupied Territories in the geography of
the world; and both bright and dark places, known and
unknown territory in the geography of the spirit. The
metaphors of my inner landscape are those of Christian
faith as experienced by me in my context of gender (female),
culture (Scottish) and calling (encouragement). But I hope
they are not exclusive. They are not meant to be so. Others
have their own metaphors for the same human experiences.
'Map is not territory.'

The markers are, of course, personal. They would not be
my story otherwise. But one of the things I have found to be
true to experience is that the personal is also political. That
is to say, the principles that determine but also liberate the
individual also operate at a corporate and cosmic level, and
vice versa. So my experience may have echoes in that of
others, and may encourage their exploring.

As part of my story, they evoke gratitude in me.
Sisterhood is a powerful reality for me, and I wish to thank
all my sisters for sharing some of my journey, but especially
Val Holtom for her readiness to risk even the shadows for
me.

Thanks also to Colin Gray for helpful and stimulating

textual comments, and to Philip Law for being a model of editorial patience and encouragement.

And thanks most of all to my children, David, Duncan and Helen, for being the people who above all ground me and accompany me on my journeyings. I could not wish for better or more delightful companions. I wish them interesting journeys of their own.

'Follow truth wherever you find it. Even if it takes you outside your preconceived ideas of God or life. Even if it takes you outside your own country into most insignificant alien places like Bethlehem. Be courageous. But concentrate on your search. Truth is one. All roads lead to home.' (George MacLeod)

KATHY GALLOWAY
MAY 1992

Dazzle and glow

'Iona is a very thin place. Only a tissue paper separates earth from heaven.'

GEORGE MACLEOD

Dazzle and glow

Did the sun ever shine so brightly again?
Was there ever again a day of such distinction?
Did the light and shadow ever compliment each other
    quite so gracefully?

On that day, I remember, I ate chicken soup,
and rode a tractor through the fields of heaven
to certify a sheep.

On that day, I put my head down on my arms and wept,
And a friend told me he loved me.

On that day, I hugged another friend in the glory-hole
beneath the stairs.

On that day, I thought that I would die of feeling,
But lived to wash the coffee-cups at midnight.

On that day, we ran like children to the door
and stood and sighed like children at the northern lights,
Painting the dark sky with a wash of silver.

On that day, mystery and mundanity embraced, and
caught me in their arms for ever more.

What a blessing of a day!
The benediction of the dazzle of water in a ditch,
And of the glow of love, and light, and night.

God's graceful moment

Morning opens wide before us
Like a door into the light
Just beyond, the day lies waiting
Ready to throw off the night,
And we stand upon its threshold
Poised to turn and take its flight.

Now the earth in all its glory
Springs to meet the rising sun,
Warms to all who walk upon it,
Cradling all that will be done,
All our labour, all our loving
Mingle and become as one.

We receive God's graceful moment,
While the day is fresh and still,
Ours to choose how we will greet it,
Ours to make it what we will.
Here is given perfect freedom,
Every hope in love to fulfil.

As we take the first step together,
Passing through the door of the day,
May the love of Christ the Creator
Give us peace in all that we say,
Heart for all that lies before us,
Grace to guide us on our way.

Song: 87 87 87   Tune: Picardy

CH3, no. 577

Narcissi in April

Late at night, moonlight and twilight were one.
Walking home, I stopped at the garden gate.
'My garden is full of stars', dancing.
Pale, shining and delicate.

Every spring after that, I waited with longing
For the starry nights.

Early ferry, winter timetable

Wind-whipped, rain-lashed,
Water dripping down our noses, boots and freezing
    fingers.
We run madly down the brae,
Feeling for the way in blackness,
Stumbling, breathless, and half-asleep.
And there we stand, forlornly huddled close for shelter.
Peering gloomily for the faintest light appearing
Like a ghost up from the sea.
Cursing, some of us, 'I wish I was in my bloody bed!'

It's here! Just time to shout or kiss goodbye,
Schoolkids dash from waiting cars, the ramp goes up.
The ferry goes, swallowed by the dark.
And we go back to bed, or work,
Cleansed, virtuous, and somehow warmed.
Our duty's done.
We have observed the 5 a.m. Monday morning
    penitential rite.

Ruth

You and I,
An unlikely combination,
And how we struggled.
Your silences, my words,
Your words, my silences.
Your hurt, my anger,
My hurt, your anger.
But something kept us going:
Your care, my stubbornness,
My care, your stubbornness,
Your love, my faith,
My love, your faith,
and we survived, and more.
We are friends,
You and I.

Last rites

A day of days, it was.
The sun had shone all summer,
And did not desert us then, although another light
    went out.
That morning it was as if it was the first day of creation.
The sky, I swear, was green, pale,
ripening into gold and blazing into scarlet.
Reflecting the earth of grass and corn
and poppies in the field.

I walked the path towards the waiting house
of anguish, dread and glory,
all our confusion, fear and weariness
built into its stone
(squeezing the stone, they would
come dripping out,
but it absorbs them, and they become
the sap that holds the dry stone tight).

We rang the bell, we said the psalm,
We sang the song, we gave the kiss.
We cooked the food, we made the beds.
We met the people—we did the needful.
That day of days, we learned together,
What was proper, owed, demanded.
It was, in its way, the first day of creation.

First rites

It was a great joke—'the North End in September'.
But that was fine, it's fine to be light-hearted
even—no, especially—about such crucial things.
And it was cold, right enough,
And we were shivering, the three of us
who waded in.
Cold, or nerves, or the wind, took my voice
and carried it away.
But it was done, the crucial thing,
The dying, living, shivering thing.

The one who died and rose said thank you.
The one who shared the weight carried it.
But you fastened up my coat when my fingers
were too cold to do it.
I stood there, meekly, like a child.
I cannot think of anything you ever did
for me
that touched me more.

'Columba would turn in his grave . . .'

Young men,
on the cusp,
between boyhood and manhood,
pose a certain problem
to knowledgeable women
of a particular age.
Don't you agree, Marl?

The long shadows of summer

The long shadows of summer
Cast their net and draw us in rejoicing.
They fall on children salt-scented from the sea
and all the busy people who tumble from the sea
and race to flavour history.
They cool the red-faced cooks and lead the desk-bound
into sunlight.

We stretch, we smile, we fall gently into daydreams,
The fretfulness and quarrels seep away.
And you and I sit on the hill, and chat,
And think of nothing much,
And watch the shadows lengthen.

Seannachie

A seannachie tells stories.
Not the bedtime kind, but ones that whistle up the
    mystery
and wrap the days with fable, so that little folk
believe they too can do daring deeds
and take on dragons, aye, and win.

A seannachie makes jokes.
And (though they're not the newest ones you've heard,
and anyway, you've heard them all before) makes folk
    smile
because the pleasure lies most deeply in the telling
and the hearing of what we all already knew,
but needed words and spirit for.

A seannachie takes risks, and clowns the tales
that most we need to hear.
He risks himself to speak to us of love
in ways that warm the heart
But do not push us to the other side of trust.

A seannachie steps through a door
and leaves it open so we can see through.
And follow through, into that land
Where magic calls, and feasts are fine,
and we, unbending, are as one.

Written for Ron Ferguson, formerly leader of the
Iona Community, on his fiftieth birthday.

Singing the Sanctus

I used to think that singing the Sanctus
on a Sunday morning
was the nearest I ever came to that place
where heaven meets earth.

'Glory to your name, O Lord most high . . .'

Small, exalted, lifted out of the constrictions
of time and space,
yet rooted by the cold of stone beneath my feet,
I understood what it meant to be raised up.

But now I think that morning coffee in the Refectory
was pretty good too.
Lingering, laughing, passing jokes and biscuits
down the polished tables.
Catching the warmth in a shaft of dusty
sunlight
and a pentecostal understanding of strange words.
It was peaceful. Mellow.
I don't know if I can live without exalted.
I *know* I can't live without mellow.

Fortunately
although they do not sing the Sanctus
in Presbyterian Glasgow,
people there drink coffee too.

A labour of love

'Who shall bear hope, who else but us?'

MARGE PIERCY

A *labour of love*

Once upon a time, in the beginning, a labour of love was
  undertaken.

It started with a sign, to show that something was about to
happen. Light came forth from the deep darkness, bright,
clear and unmistakable.
And it was very good.

At the second time, the waters were broken. At first, they
gushed, then they dried to a trickle, and a space was
created. It was exactly the right size. By now, the creation
was well under way.
And it was very good.

At the third time, a cradle was made ready. It was
comfortable and beautiful and waiting. And food was
prepared, issuing sweetly and warmly and in precisely the
right measure from the being of the labourer.
And it was very good.

At the fourth time, rhythm was established. Ebbing and
flowing, contracting and expanding, pain and joy, sun and
moon, beginning and ending. The labour of love
progressed.
And it was very good.

At the fifth time, there was ceaseless activity. Fluttering
like the wings of the dove, humming like the murmur of
the dragonfly, swimming like the darting golden fish,
wriggling like the lithe serpent, leaping like the flashing
deer, surging like the mighty lion.
And it was very good.

At the sixth time, there was a momentary, endless hesitation. Then a child was born. And the child looked like the one who had given it life. The child too was born with the power to create and to make decisions and to love.
The labourer looked at all that had been accomplished, and rejoiced, for it was very good.

At the seventh time, the labour was finished. The task was complete.
And the labourer rested, for she was very, very tired.

Nice girls

Nice girls don't go out in the street alone at night,
Nice girls don't go into bars;
Nice girls don't go out with lots of different men,
Nice girls don't take lifts in cars.
But nice girls don't mind Uncle Tom with his hand on
   their knee,
Nice girls never complain,
Nice girls don't mind being kissed by a drunk,
Nice girls all know it's a game.

Nice girls don't make approaches to men they've just met,
Nice girls just leave it up to you,
Nice girls don't tell you the way that they feel,
Nice girls will fake what isn't real.
Nice girls all know just how far they can go with you,
Nice girls know when to say no.
And if you don't hear, or ignore, or don't stop,
Nice girls know you are made so.

Nice girls don't argue or shout or get mad,
Nice girls don't talk about rights,
Nice girls are pretty and loving and kind,
Nice girls don't get into fights.
And nice girls don't mind being girls till they're fifty,
Nice girls just love being nice,
Nice girls know what they have to do to get it right,
Nice girls will pay any price.

I cannot call you Lord

I cannot call you Lord
With undivided heart,
For though my love would stronger be
It cannot take the part

Of those who seek to rule
By force or evil word
And justify their deeds of pride
As from a Sovereign Lord.

Nor can I yet forgive
A Lord Omnipotent
Who sanctions women, children, prey
As if such things were meant.

And if I should attempt
To call you Lord of Hosts
From every battlefield rise up
A million slaughtered ghosts.

I cannot find the word
To fit this woman's hour,
That lets me praise the power of love
Not fear the love of power.

Yet Jesus *is* my Lord,
The Life for all who seek,
The Liberator of the poor,
The Servant of the weak.

But he with you is One;
Before my heart must break,
O God, who are *not* man, help me
Find word, for this man's sake.

Song: S.M.   Tune: Carlisle; Rise Up, O Men of God
CH3, no. 477

I danced in the Kremlin

I danced in the Kremlin one evening in June,
There were two thousand of me, and I was one,
I was black, I was white, I was golden and tan,
And I danced with myself, never looked for a man.

I wore cotton and denim, I wore satin and lace,
I was carefree and girlish, I had lines on my face,
Was the mother of children, was a bride and a nun,
Was a teacher, a farmer, and I carried a gun.

I danced in a circle and I held my own hand,
I sang my own song in a strange unknown land,
Though my voice sounded foreign, the music was fine,
For a few hours that evening, the Kremlin was mine.

And the men in dark suits who stared while I danced,
Could not move as I whirled round and held them
      entranced,
They blushed and they smiled, when I gave them a flower,
For a few hours the Kremlin was quite in my power.

How often they dance in that place I don't know,
I imagine that Congress would never end so,
But it's hard to stop dancing when once you've begun,
I'm dancing there now, the two thousand and one.

In Senegal

In Senegal the women grow like handsome, upright trees,
Their roots go deep into the earth, they sway against the
  breeze,
They stand so tall and strong and proud, they stretch to
  touch the sun,
And decked in golden foliage, they give shade to
  everyone.

In Canada the women fly like wild geese soaring high,
They cross the plains and mountains in an endless open
  sky,
They carve their flight path fearlessly, together they are
  strong,
And when their leaders tire, the others carry them along.

In India the women glide like swans upon a lake,
Their stately elegance revealed in every move they make,
And though their necks may droop beneath the weight
  of faithfulness
Their grace will touch the lifelong day with feathery
  caress.

In Russia the women flow like water in a stream,
They carry many loads along in patient, endless dream,
The ripple of their voice is like a waterfall at play,
Though stone their bed, the river's flow will wear the
  stone away.

In Salvador the women fight like tigers caught at bay,
They turn to face the predators who on their children
  prey,
And for their young they stand their ground and give
  their every breath,
And all their skill and all their pain give courage until
  death.

The love of this land

It's not in the mountains and glens, though beautiful they
 are for sure,
Nor the myths and the songs of the past, though they also
 have their allure,
Nor even the causes for pride, the struggles we've had to
 endure,
It's the women of Scotland who move me, and give me
 the love of this land.

In forest and cave they gave birth, in hovel and tenement
 slum,
They worked for their bairns to survive, they worked for
 the good times to come.
And when all the soldiers marched by, they marched to a
 different drum,
It's the women of Scotland who move me, and give me
 the love of this land.

For when the landstealers came, with their guns and their
 sheep and their fire,
The women stood strong to resist, and screamed for the
 funeral pyre
That burned them right down to the sea, the victims of
 honour for hire,
It's the women of Scotland who move me, and give me
 the love of this land.

They took to the streets in rent-strikes, and miners' wives
 marched for their men,
They marched to get suffrage for women, and for safety
 to walk on their own,
They marched at Coulport and Faslane, to say: 'Nuclear
 war, never again.'
It's the women of Scotland who move me, and give me
 the love of this land.

From factory and office and mill, when the long working
    week was done,
From harbours where poor fisher lasses found their name
    used to put women down,
They'd stream home to put on their glad rags, and go out
    for a night on the town,
It's the women of Scotland that move me, and give me
    the love of this land.

There's a body of knowledge and wisdom from mother to
    daughter passed on
Of how to get by on a little, what to do when your man's
    drunk, or gone,
For where would we be without mothers, and sisters and
    friends to lean on,
It's the women of Scotland that move me, and give me
    the love of this land.

This land's been well served by its women, though you
    wouldn't ken that from a book,
Nor from its places of power, where they get scarcely
    a look,
But it's time to start listening to women, their story we
    must understand,
It's the women of Scotland who move me, and give me
    the love of this land.

The love burning deep

'. . . but when I say, "I will forget the Lord
and no longer speak in his name",
then your message is like a fire burning deep
within me . . .'
I try my best to hold it in,
but can no longer keep it back.

JEREMIAH 20.9

Wrestling with God

Get off my back, God.
Take your claws out of my shoulder.
I'd like to throw you off
like I would brush off some particularly repellent insect!

Sometimes I get the feeling that if I could turn round
    quick enough
I would see you
grinning at me,
full of glee, plotting, scheming, devious, challenging.

The hell with all this rubbish about fire and storm
and still, quiet waters.
I've got your number.
I've unmasked you.

I'd like to throw you off
like I would brush off
some particularly repellent insect.

You're a daemon!

Unfortunately, you seem to have this great attachment
    to me.

Actually, being honest, I know in my heart
I'd miss you if you weren't there,
leering at me, reminding me of
death and dread and destiny,
winding me up and puncturing
my pretensions.

I know, with a sinking feeling in my gut
that all the best of me —
the fire and storm, and even, now and then, still waters,
are born out of the death-defying struggle
that we wage,
my dearest daemon.

The life of the world

Oh the life of the world is a joy and a treasure
unfolding in beauty the green growing tree,
the changing of seasons in mountain and valley,
the stars and the bright restless sea.

Oh the life of the world is a fountain of goodness
overflowing in labour and passion and pain,
in the sound of the city and the silence of wisdom
in the birth of a child once again.

Oh the life of the world is the source of our healing,
it rises in laughter and wells up in song,
it springs from the care of the poor and the broken
and refreshes where justice is strong.

So give thanks for the life and give love to the Maker,
and rejoice in the gift of the bright risen Son,
and walk in the peace and the power of the Spirit
till the days of our living are done.

Song

SGP, no. 87

Tune: Life of the World
(Ian Galloway)

The story

From creation's start, there has been a story
told from age to age of the maker's glory;
painted in the sky, sung in joy and sadness,
acted out in love, raged against in madness.

Though the love was there, we would not believe it,
blinded by our fears, we could not receive it.
Pride, oppression, hate, ride the world uncaring;
in the lust for life, we would die despairing.

Listen for the voice, it has never vanished,
though to death's dark night, we had thought it banished;
hear it through the guns, from the prisons ringing,
from the long-denied, songs of freedom singing.

Hear it from the poor, crying for each other,
from the sister scorned, reaching to a brother,
from the wounded heart, touching us in pity,
hear it from the cross, raised outside the city.

Everyone who hears with the heart and spirit
knows the story true, life we shall inherit;
what we give away shall return completed,
so the song goes on, evermore repeated.

Glory be to God, mystery in giving,
glory be to Jesus, one with us in living,
glory to the Spirit, hurt among us mending,
trinity of life, in the life unending,
glory be to God.

Song: 56 56 D   Tune: Can Ye Ower Frae France
                       (Scottish Traditional Melody)

SGP, no. 30

To the baby God

You are dearer than death
you are gentler than breathing,
in the smallness of being,
in the nearness of you,
in the movement of limbs
in the stillness of sleeping
in the anguish of care
is the wonder of you.

You are precious to me
there is nobody like you,
every day holds delight
as I greet it with you.
What the future will bring
I have no way of telling,
but I trust you to show me
all the wonder of you.

I am filled with such awe
for I know my own weakness,
How can I do what's best
for the treasure of you?
But you give me your love
without question or doubting
so I know you'll forgive
that's the wonder of you.

Go to sleep now my darling,
even you need your resting,
I will care by your side
for the world that you love.
You have given your life,
so frail and so trusting
into my human hands,
that's the wonder of you.

Song: 6767   Tune: Brahms Lullaby

Sometimes I cry

Sometimes I cry when I think of the child
born in a stable, no room anywhere
growing to live in a world cold with grief and shame
dying in agony, nailed there by fear.

Sometimes I pray when I think of the child
born to be human in weakness and care,
growing to stand with the poor and the prisoner
dying to raise them in freedom to share.

Sometimes I laugh when I think of the child
born without name on the edge of the town
growing in powerlessness, changer of images,
dying derided and mocked as a clown.

Sometimes I tremble when I think of the child
born out of mystery, starlight and sign,
maker of miracles out of reality,
raising them up till the end of all time.

But sometimes I sing when I think of the child
born out of joy and obedience and pain,
growing to touch human living with ecstasy
dying to show us that love lives again.

Song   Tune: Summertime (freely)

The good I would

The good I would I do not do
so much gets in the way,
I hurt the people that I love
with wounding things I say.
I do not mean to make it so,
but tiredness, fear and scorn
wear down my will, reduce me, till
my goodness dies stillborn.

The good I would I do not do
my deeds don't match my words,
I talk of love, self-sacrifice,
but seek instead rewards.
I want to serve the poor and hurt,
engage in justice' cause,
but turn away, bored or put-out
because there's no applause.

I need your love to draw me on,
and give my kindness voice.
I need your strength to raise me up
to make the better choice.
I need your mercy telling me
that I can try again.
And your acceptance holding out
the joy that comes through pain.

Song: DCM irregular   Tune: Kingsfold

CH3, no. 212

Liberator Lord

To those whose lives are bitter, the poor and dispossessed
your word is one of justice, of balances redressed,
the riches of creation a commonwealth possessed.
May your spirit be upon us, our Liberator Lord.

To those who live in bondage of body and of mind
who are prisoners of ignorance or the hatred of their kind
your word is one of liberty, the captive to unbind.
May your spirit be upon us, our Liberator Lord.

To those whose eyes are blinded, who will or dare not see
your word is calling softly, come, face reality
and find in it the dearest truth, your lives will precious be.
May your spirit be upon us, our Liberator Lord.

To those who know the anguish of love that cannot flower
whose race or class or gender define another's power,
your word is one of freedom to grow and not to cower.
May your spirit be upon us, our Liberator Lord.

You have spoken through the prophets and saints of
  history
through the sobbing of the voiceless and the groans of
  the unfree
and your voice is still proclaiming, 'now, you must speak
  for me.'
May your spirit be upon us, our Liberator Lord.

Song: Irregular   Tune: Cormac

CH3, no. 365

Sing for God's glory

Sing for God's glory that colours the dawn of creation
racing across the sky trailing bright clouds of elation
sun of delight succeeds the velvet of night
warming the earth's exultation.

Sing for God's power that shatters the chains that would
    bind us
searing the darkness of fear and despair that could
    blind us
touching our shame with love that will not lay blame
reaching out gently to find us.

Sing for God's justice disturbing each easy illusion
tearing down tyrants and putting our pride to confusion
lifeblood of right, resisting evil and slight
offering freedom's transfusion.

Sing for God's saints who have travelled faith's journey
    before us
who in our weariness give us their hope to restore us
in them we see the new creation to be
spirit of love made flesh for us.

Song: 14 14 14   Tune: Lobe Den Herren

CH3, no. 9

Charity?

Do not offer me your money
if that's all you have to give,
though my clothes may be in tatters
and my flesh too frail to live.
For my dignity will clothe me,
it does not depend on you,
God-intended, God-revealing,
it will let my spirit through.

Do not offer me your pity
if that's all you have to spare,
though I'm spat upon and taunted
and nobody seems to care.
For the light that shines within me
reflects the glory that is God
and although I walk in darkness
it cannot extinguish God.

Do not offer me your answers
if that's all that you can do,
though you see me as a problem
in the unemployment queue.
I am person, not statistic,
my life is pleasing to the Lord,
by that grace I am of value,
holy, human, is the word.

Do not offer me your comfort
if you cannot give your love,
though I'm bleeding, broken, helpless
caught whichever way I move.
Oh, awake your heart to courage
do not soothe it into sleep,
for to live in faith is costly,
and indifference is cheap.

Song: 87 87 D   Tune: Converse

SGP, no. 115

The spirit is moving in my heart

The spirit is moving in my heart
the spirit is moving in my heart
It's moving me to love and share
to work for freedom everywhere
the spirit is moving in my heart

The spirit moved the people to the promised land
the spirit raised up prophets who would take a stand
it spoke a language everyone could understand
the spirit was moving in my heart

The spirit moved the Lord to heal in Galilee
it moved him to a cross to die on Calvary
it raised him from the tomb to say, 'come follow me'
the spirit was moving in their hearts

The spirit moved my sister to a prison cell
she didn't want a bomb to blow the world to hell
she knows that love is meant for enemies as well
the spirit is moving in her heart

The spirit moved my brother where the poor folk stay
and share the weary struggle for their bread each day
and learn the need of loving that's the kingdom way
the spirit is moving in his heart

The spirit's moving folk to see what they can do
it's moving in Managua and Soweto too
the spirit moves in everything that's just and true
the spirit is moving in their hearts

The spirit doesn't care about the wrong you've done
the spirit isn't proud, it's meant for everyone
let the spirit move you, your new life's begun
the spirit is moving in our hearts

She comes

She comes with mother's kindnesses
and bends to touch and heal.
She gives her heart away in love
for those who cannot feel.

She comes with lover's tenderness
to answer love's appeal.
She gives her body with her heart
to make her passion real.

She comes with worker's faithfulness
to sow and reap and spin.
She bends her back in common task
to gather harvest in.

She comes with artist's joyfulness
to make and shape and spin.
She gives her hands and from them grows
a free and lovely thing.

She comes, a child in humbleness
and trust is in her eyes.
And through them all of life appears
in wondering surprise.

She comes with sister's carefulness
strong to support and bind.
Her voice will speak for justice' sake
and peace is in her mind.

She comes with power like the night
and glory like the day.
Her reign is in the heart of things
Oh come to us and stay.

Song: CM   Tune: Martyrs
CH3, no. 7

Seas roll back

Seas roll back and mountains tremble
and rain will dance upon the desert
the rose will grow in splendour bright.
Dawn is born of darkness' labour
and shadowed sorrow long in waiting
no more may fear the tender night.
For Love has left her throne
and comes to claim her own
her beloved.
All living things in joy embrace
to see the glory of her face.

Every hate and every hunger
will flee before her holy anger
and healing every hurt will find.
Every wrong with justice mending
she walks abroad in pity tending
the aching heart of humankind.
For Love has come to earth
inviting us to birth
new creation.
Both men and women, flesh and flower
are split with her emerging power.

Come and dance, come shout with gladness
come leave your shame, shake off your sadness
and make your peace with all that's past.
We may rightly know each other
and rightly live as sister, brother,
in freedom reaching out at last.
For Love is moving through,
her spirit draws us to
true communion.
To shake and shatter every bond
and find our holy common ground.

Song: 898 D 66 4 88   Tune: Wachet Auf

CH3, no. 315

Written for the Hallowing Service of the Iona Community.

The love burning deep

Come out of the darkness, come out of the shadow
come out of the endless night,
all you who are poor now, all you who are broken
all you who are bowed by fight.
Come into the light of God's sacred intention
come under the shelter of her hand,
here you may find riches, here you may find healing,
here now you may rise and stand.

Come out from your prisons, come out from your ghettoes,
come out from behind your walls,
leave all your distinctions, leave all your derisions,
and answer her when she calls.
For she is your end as she was your beginning
she is the desire of all your days,
in her love is fullness, in her love is wholeness,
holy will be all her ways.

No more will you rest now, no more take your ease now,
no more let your life go by,
always you will seek her, forever desire her
until the day you die.
Her love will consume you, blazing deep within you
burning away all that is not true,
until you embrace her, in flesh and in spirit
holy you and wholly you.

Song   Tune: Sing of the Lord's Goodness

SGP, no. 95

Christ of Scotland

He walks among the yellow and the grey.
Grey of stone and slate and steely rivers
running through grey towns where steel ran yesterday,
and grey mists lifting where the coming day
delivers grey-edged intimations of
a grey mortality,
and a shadier morality.
Here, poverty and pain are dirty-fingered currency
in the market-place of souls,
and stunted possibility hobbles on the bleeding stumps
of legs hacked off from under it.
Here, in the grey forgotten wasteland
that is not fate or accident or fecklessness
but just the grey, inevitable result
of choices made,
and burdens shifted,
and costs externalised out of the magic circle
of prosperity,
here, he walks.

But in his heart, he carries yellow.
Yellow for the daffodils that surge across the banks
of railway lines.
Yellow for the crocuses that parade in Charlotte Square.
Yellow for the primroses that gleam in crevices of island
    rock.
Yellow for the irises that wave from glittering ditches.
Yellow for the broom that flashes fire across a thousand
    summer hills.

Yellow for the barren land cloaked in winter snow,
awaiting yellow springtime's sun
to kiss it into bloom.
He carries yellow in his heart.
Held high like the lion raised upon the terraces.
Yellow for courage.
Yellow for beauty.
Yellow for resistance.
Yellow for love.
Yellow to obliterate the grey.
He walks, yellow, in the grey.

Let us be different

'Removing all traces of racism from our relations means affirming that we are different and that we shall remain different.'

EDGAR PISANI

In transit: the world

How travel broadens one's horizons!
How else would one meet such a strange variety of
   humankind
sitting, time suspended, in stuffy transit lounges,
or hurtling through the dark
chasing dawns and dusks in swift succession,
flashing by the sun and moon and stars;
engaging in polite discussion
of jobs and homes and the weather.

That girl in Amsterdam, the one with such long hair,
I thought that she was Japanese, but she was
born in Sweden, and lived there all her life.
Now she is nervous, going to the home of her ancestors,
because she cannot speak the language very well.

And the woman with the baby on the flight;
she is a nurse, is Chinese from Taiwan.
But now she lives in Wiesbaden, in Germany,
selling flowers with her German husband
caring for her placid, beautiful child.
She is going to surprise her parents at the Chinese
   New Year.

And in Taipei, the tiny, shell-like, fragile Thai,
married to a US sailor in Japan.
How does it feel to know both the prejudice of white
   America
and the resentment of exploited, militarised Asia?
No wonder that she looks like she might break.

En route to Okinawa there was Nancy,
elderly, ungainly, sweat shining on her nose,
coming from Manila with a pile of paper bags.
Kindness and uncertainty combined
in sharp Australian calm and businesslike exterior.

The old man with the leathered face
grows Christmas trees in Californian sun,
and wanders restlessly round the world alone,
pretending not to know the clucking group
of fellow countrymen and women
marching noisily through terminals in dreadful clothes.

The German woman, coming home to West Berlin
from visiting her son in Tokyo
was worldly-wise and rich and very charming
in a kind of Central European way,
as if to say, all this I have seen and done,
and that, and nothing shocks me any more.

In terminals across the world
like looks for like, familiar tongues and colours,
and like gets wider as unlike gets deeper.
In Europe, one looks for Scots or Irish, or, at the least,
    English.
In Asia, any western-like will do.
And Germans, Dutch, Norwegian, sink thankfully into
    English
as if it was a native (black American as welcome as a
    white) tongue!
All this, not, I sense, from racism, or dislike even,
more often from anxiety or lostness, or simply fear.
And travellers alone make brief, intense relationships
with meaning far beyond their worth.
Then wish each other well, and part, and pass
to gate 1 or 8, or out into the timed and weathered world.

Tonight in Tokyo

Tonight in Tokyo, you asked me to help you.
You were worried about your ticket,
And, uncertain, with that faint, indefinable, attractive
    seediness
of brown-eyed men,
I found you vulnerable, and appealing.

Tonight in Taipei, you asked me to stay the night
    with you,
Out of desire mingling with loneliness, I suppose.
But you seemed to ask more in hope than in expectation,
Telling me that 'I looked married',
As if 'always thinking of him'.

Tomorrow you will be in Manila and I in Amsterdam,
And I will try to imagine what your life is like,
An Iranian in the Philippines, exiled from home,
And regret a little that I did not meet you
on the outward flight, when I had time to spare.

Over coffee

People tell me terrible things over coffee,
and I don't know what to do.
If I say nothing, will they think that I don't care,
that I am indifferent to their words.
But if I try to speak, I am afraid
that what I say will sound clichéd,
debased or trite or uninformed.
So there I sit, playing with my cup,
stumbling, muttering, wanting very much
to say something that will honour the immensity
of what they say.

Heiwa

*('Heiwa' is the Japanese word for peace. It is made up of
two characters, the one meaning harmony, and the other
meaning equality.)*

See the children born of sorrow,
Born to face a world gone wrong;
Shine the sun of justice on them,
Deliver them to meet the dawn.
Shine the light of freedom's morning
In the darkened prison cell,
Give them honour in their struggle
To bring heaven out of hell.

See the children of the atom,
Shattered limbs and twisted faces,
Locked within their hearts they carry
Burning bodies, ruined places.
Heed their plea and hear their story,
Swear by their undying pain,
Hiroshima, Nagasaki,
Never again, never again.

See the children of the city
Sweat for fourteen hours a day,
Sell their labour, sell their bodies
For a bare subsistence pay.
In the rubbish and the shanties,
Poisoned by the factories' rain,
Bangkok, Bhopal, Minnemata,
Never again, never again.

See the children of the ocean,
Rooted from ancestral lands,
For the safety of the powerful,
Threatened death at foreign hands.
Nuclear mining, dumping, testing,
Linking in a deadly chain,
Muraroa, Marshall Islands
Never again, never again.

See the children of the prisons,
Breakers of the laws of fear,
Stand before the might of tyrants,
With the threat of torture near.
In their courage grows the freedom
That will break oppression's chains,
Rangoon, Beijing, Mindanao,
Never again, never again.

On Yom Kippur

On Yom Kippur, he walked for several miles
to outside of the city walls
to come and talk to us,
and, I suspect, to keep faith with his friend.

He talked with clarity and fluency about the 'victim'
    psyche of his people,
and how Saddam had put a greater barrier between the
    peaceseekers
than they had yet encountered.
He said his son, patrolling the West Bank,
if ordered by his officer to shoot
would, of course, obey.
And he requested that the Palestinians
should withhold their anger
for the sake of greater trust.

This is a source of deep division, naturally.
Comparable, perhaps, to Western Christians,
blood-stained from the Holocaust
and even now, trailing the sting of anti-semitism in their
    tail,
requesting that Israelis
should refrain from occupation and injustice
and the blind eye turned.

People do not do what once was done to them
because they're bad, or just to be unkind.
It's just, 'it's my turn now for happiness, for
peace, for some security. I'm owed it, and this time,
someone else must pay the price. I've paid enough.'

Where is there hope in such a karma?

Perhaps a glimmer.
Noam and Souhail still talk.
Still, there is desire, in spite of everything,
to agree at least in disagreement.

'If your enemy asks you to go one mile,
go the extra mile with him.'
Today, at least, he walked the extra mile.

'. . . He is at home here . . .'

(for Robin)

It is a long way
from Yarrow Valley to the Jordan
Valley.
Miles, language, climate, politics, time,
create vast distances between them.
But you leap these at a bound,
(having made friendship, vision,
humour and respect
your giant's boots)
and land
on common ground.

The feminist dialectic

In Mauritius, there are many beautiful trees.
Feathery filaos; drooping, fruit-laden lychees,
cassias, the Indian laburnum, shedding golden petals
like confetti on the dusty roads;
the bandamier, fragrant, lofty almond,
standing sentinel in cool green swathes around
the curving silver sands of secret seas.
And most of all, the flame-flamboyant tree,
throwing its impressionistic streaks of scarlet
across a tropical horizon; Monet meets Gauguin.

Many beautiful trees, but so far,
though I have been alert
and on the look-out,
no drunken Glasgow poets, no,
not even one
never mind a half-dozen.
And this I miss,
for one of the advantages of inhabiting
the feminist dialectic —
both/and, not either/or —
is that one need never choose,
nor even make comparisons,
but on the contrary,
can simply appreciate them both
and bless the world that holds
such strange and wonderful phenomena
as trees and drunken Glasgow poets.

A respectful response to a reported quote from Kenneth White, the Scottish poet and Professor of Poetry at the Sorbonne, that there is more poetry in one tree than in half a dozen drunken Glasgow poets.

A different order of creation

Now I see skinny lizards, skiting through the grass
and darting geckos,
naked with the vulnerability of rubber bands,
and tiny, twitchy frogs as curious as babies.
I have grown intimate with ants
and carefree with cockroaches.
I hear the whizzing of the dragonfly
above the whirring of the fan.
I have learned to apprehend mosquitoes,
and sat transfixed while butterflies
with wings more beautiful than peacock damask
visited my blue bag time and time again.

A whole and complicated order of creation
imposed itself upon my gaze
while I sat still and drank my coffee
in the garden.
Or rather, I should say,
I opened my eyes and saw it,
opened my ears and heard it,
narrowed my field and selected it.
Together we changed me.

Behind the wires

Look around you, can't you see what you're missing,
Look around you, open your eyes;
There's a whole world of loving and meeting
In a place where hostility dies.

Oh, I know that you don't mean to hurt me,
You only want to protect what you've got,
But don't you know that the best way to lose it
Is to think that your freedom can be bought.

If you shut out your spirit of adventure,
If you close up your heart from within,
You build walls to keep out the danger
And find that you've locked yourself in.

I believe that peace is what we're after,
But we've drawn up the lines for a war;
Surrender in trust to one another,
It's the only thing worth fighting for.

So come out from behind your fences,
You're in a war that no one can win,
Take a chance, lay down your defences,
If I pull down the wire from the outside
Please won't you pull it down from within.

*Written for the women of the Greenham Common
Peace Camp.*

Do not retreat

Do not retreat into your private world,
That place of safety, sheltered from the storm
Where you may tend your garden, seek your soul,
And rest with loved ones where the fire burns warm.

To tend a garden is a precious thing,
But dearer still the one where all may roam,
The weeds of poison, poverty and war
Demand your care, who call the earth your home.

To seek your soul, it is a precious thing,
But you will never find it on your own,
Only among the clamour, threat and pain
Of other people's need will love be known.

To rest with loved ones is a precious thing,
But peace of mind exacts a higher cost,
Your children will not rest and play in quiet,
While they still hear the crying of the lost.

Do not retreat into your private world,
There are more ways than firesides to keep warm,
There is no shelter from the rage of life,
So meet its eye, and dance within the storm.

Song: 10 10 10   Tune: Sursum Corda

CH3, no. 68

Going over

You have burned your bridges.

You have passed through the gate marked 'no return'
and for you, there is no going back.
No going back to the security of the known, familiar
    house,
to the well-worn dispensations and the threadbare
    coverings.

Now you are out there in uncharted territory
heavy with threat and shadows not yet entered.
The risks are high, and yet you strike out boldly,
guided only by unwavering conviction
and the longing for the true centre of the land.
This is what it means to do a new thing.

And yet, you travel lightly.
You are abandoned, given up in all things
to the task that lies ahead.
Therefore, you may be exactly who you are.
You have inhabited yourself,
you are at home,
and home is where you are,
even if it is the desert.
No one can dispossess you of your own in-dwelling.
This is what it means to be free.

We stand, one foot upon the bridge,
wondering if we too have the courage to go over
and strike the match behind us.

Singing my blues away

If I sing out my pain, will it go away,
If I open my heart, will the sorrow stray,
When I sob my story in a musical way,
I'm singing my blues away.

Well I've talked it through till my throat is dry,
I have analysed every look and sigh,
I've examined the how and the where and why,
Now I'm singing my blues away.

I have been advised, but the ache's still in place,
And I've tried being brave with a smile on my face,
I'm tired of feeling that empty space,
So I'm singing my blues away.

My heart's been sealed with a lock and key,
And the only one who can release it is me,
I'm going to cut out that pain and set it free
By singing my blues away.

There will be peace between us

In laughter I will find you,
So many joys I will have shared with you,
They will become the measure of our time,
And there will be love between us
And there will be peace between us.

In tears I will find you,
So many times I will have cried for you,
I will offer you my song to ease your pain
And there will be love between us
And there will be peace between us.

In anger I will find you,
So many times I will have hated you,
But your tenderness will disarm me,
And there will be love between us
And there will be peace between us.

In losing I will find you,
So many times I will be without you,
But the things that you have given will not leave me,
And there will be love between us,
And there will be peace between us.

Gestalt of intimacy

It comes in different ways.

The scent of eucalyptus fills the warm night air.
The sounds are unfamiliar.
There is a courtyard, stars, tall gins upon the table,
and laughter sings a private song.
In this land of heightened passions,
heightened senses, heightened tensions,
we have felt in every part alive.
Fear and fury, love, death, beauty, courage
charge us . . .
exhaustion unwinds into exhilaration,
humour, relaxation.
We draw a circle round us.
It completes itself.
Intensity brings intimacy.

Or, in the darkness, hand-held,
where nobody can see
what is not seeable by light
and night is thick to deaden
whispers, rustlings, half-held breaths that transparent day
strains through with all the clarity and outrage
of raspberries seeping through white muslin.
Enclosed in stealth,
secrecy brings intimacy.

The sharp eroticism of words
plays through us;
we fence, stab, lunge, and send them spinning
on our points to glitter, hang and fall
to land in slightly different forms.
They lie like jewelled heaps.
We toss them to and fro just for the fierce joy
of the play.

the nervous, guarded daring of a cut
that flashes flesh from bone
and shows us something previously unseen.
This game is satisfying;
within the circle, its clashes spark
like diamond shards of provocation.
But our swords are tipped, and so
we cannot kill each other.
Combat brings intimacy.

The bleak unfolding tale commands attentiveness,
and pain brings forth compassion like the rain
brings green to ruined, smouldering hillsides.
Desire and pride and anguish are a potent combination
in any conjugation.
Secrets shift around; what was hidden
is revealed, only to mask,
in turn, another openness.
The pool of candlelight casts long shadows.
Intimation brings intimacy.

I cannot do it.

I cannot stay within the magic circle,
putting on safety like an enfolding velvet armour,
although the ache of wanting gnaws me like a hunger.
I cannot complete when completion means exclusion.
Outside the courtyard, in the night,
where one false move means death,
the shadows beckon.
There is no excitement in this danger,
only dread-filled hope, and possibility.
Here, where the space that is not joined
exposes wounds, the memory of violation,
chilled, defenceless flesh,
love is something else.

To face the slow remorseless drip of indignity beyond the
   courtyard
and not be drowned by it;
to meet the ghosts that haunt the night
and to befriend them;
to turn, and face the enemy and embrace him,
not once, but with a thousand faces for a thousand days;
to walk into the shadows and explore them.
This is love.

I will not substitute the gestalt of intimacy
for the gestalt of love.
I will not.
I choose.

Let us be different

Let us be different,
Let us not be the same,
You will be you, I will be me,
Each of us has our own name.

You do things your way,
In the light you have found,
You must be true to what you know,
And stand on your own ground.

Until we can learn
To honour each other,
To hear and know what makes us real
We can't love one another.

But when that time comes,
Though many the flowers,
From different roots, we shall be shown
That one earth is ours.

Coming to Jerusalem

'The historic story of Christ, the outside story of
Christ, suddenly emerges as the inside story of
yourself — and it's this inner story, this inner
parallel, that really makes the Bible inspired, so
that to your condition it becomes the
living word of God.'

GEORGE MACLEOD

'Only forgiveness breaks the law of karma'

RAIMUNDO PANIKKAR

Sunday: Coming to Jerusalem

We come with high hopes,
trailing expectations,
our own and others.
We come by many different means;
on foot, on horseback, some by sea, and some,
more lately, with removal vans.
We bear the weight of many histories;
strange lands, exotic memories, the scent of cumin
and the brightness of a Neapolitan sky.
We ask the questions in pentecostal tongues —
Gaelic, Irish, Cantonese,
in Yiddish, Polish, Urdu and Punjabi —
'who' and 'how' and 'what' and 'why'.
That's if we have the time and energy
to ask at all.
We come in exile from the jeer, the sneer, the midnight
    knock,
the dogs, the wire, the gas.
Or earlier, we run from fire and famine, so our children
    won't eat grass
and die like rabbits retching in a ditch.
We come because the old ways have departed
and sheep now reign where once the children played.
Old loyalties betrayed, old verities found wanting,
old certainties upturned, we come, cast out of Eden.

And tread our way among the crowds, in fear and
    fascination
of the city and its multitudes of possibilities.
Do we want to be here?
Perhaps.
But here we are regardless.
Seeking better times, polishing our hopes,
nursing our wounds, hiding all our doubts.

And somewhere in the corner of our minds,
suspicion flies to warn us that the gap between
our hopes and their fulfilment is somewhat large—
and slides away again.
All we have left behind us (or think we have);
the terror, rage, betrayal, death,
lie also in our future, here, among the shops and houses
and the heedless crowds.
There is no route that leads us back to Eden.
We must go on, and seek a more unvarnished,
    unacclaimed reality.
There are no shortcuts—this road's going all the way.

Catholic or Protestant,
Jew or Moslem,
Hindu or Buddhist,
agnostic or atheist,
it's all the same.
We're all coming to Jerusalem.
This is where there's nowhere left to run.
This is where we stand, and walk and fall, and (will we?)
    rise again.
There it is.
Pictured in the red and green and gold.
Welcome to Jerusalem.
City of . . . .

Monday: Up against the wall

Up against the wall

Da da da da da!

That's the sound of machine-gun fire, staccato,
slamming you against the wall
and crumpling you down to the ground.

That's what I'd do to you,
you people who whinge about trivialities,
about your food, your comforts, your things, your
    precious privacy.

That's what I'd do to you,
you people who are wrapped in your smiling superiority
you people who know all the answers and patronize
    the stumbling questioners.

That's what I'd do to you,
you people who are not serious about the suffering of
    the poor,
you who seek a soothing spiritual massage
or seek the safety of the sidelines to throw stones from.

You should thank God, you people,
that thoughts can't kill.
Otherwise you'd be spreadeagled, lifeless, on the carpet.

I would topple the idols, and you people who raise
    them up.
I would fling them down with fury.
And you must admit, there is a glorious finality about
    my anger,
even if a few innocent bystanders get caught by a ricochet.

My solution has enormous potential.
My anger has a huge scope.
It is almost unequalled as a cause of dispatch,
and has no need to be proportionate to the offence.

Of course, it does require of me, in my imagination
   at least,
that I should cease to be merely human.
I would be god-like in my anger.

O God, the problem with my anger unleashed
is the same as that of my love tied up.
It puts me at the centre
and is the greatest idolatry.

Turn me over, Jesus,
Drive me out.
Cast me from your temple
Away from the house of prayer back to the streets and
   alleyways
Until my love grows at least equal to my anger
If not greater.

Tuesday: Author-ity

Some people want to eat their words.
Me, I'd rather regurgitate mine.
Throw them up. Flush them down the toilet.
Big words.
Long words.
Important words.
Poisonous words.
Difficult words.
'In' words.
In the words of the song, 'I'm so sick of words'.
'. . . just let me say this . . .'
'. . . if I could get a word in edgeways . . .'
'. . . you never listen to a word I say . . .'
'. . . though I speak with the tongues of men and
   angels . . .'
Passwords
Cover words
Swear words
Lying-in-your-teeth words

But without words
there are no stories.
Even the artist in the cave
had a word
to distinguish 'horse' from 'bull.'
and so translate the images distinctly.

Perhaps the key is in the way you use them.
Is it kind?
Is it necessary?
Is it true?
To answer these requires the use of many more words
discerning words
listening words
evaluating words

'In the beginning was the Word. And the Word became
   flesh . . . .'

I want to write my story in flesh.
Embody it.
Incarnate it.

Wednesday: What I know now . . .

It is the ache, the ache of weariness
It is the longing, the longing for peace,
It is the separation, the separation from others,
and from you.

I know the ache of weariness — tired by the decisions that
 lie behind me
— fearful of the choices that
 lie before me
— wishing only for it all to be
 resolved, to reach an end
I offer you my decisions, and my fear, and my wish for
 easy endings.
I offer them in trust, for they are safe with you.
You understand my ache.

I know the longing for peace — to get away from the
 endless demands of people
— to lay down the burdens of
 responsibility
— to escape the obligation of
 always having to be
 patient and explain.
I offer you the demands, the burdens, the obligations.
I offer them in trust, for they are safe with you.
You understand my longing.

I know the separation — feeling alone in a roomful of
 people
— needing a friend in the struggle
— wanting more, yet not quite
 knowing what
I offer you my aloneness, my struggle, my incompleteness
I offer them in trust, for they are safe with you.
You understand my separation.

Forgive me that my offering is so little.
I would have it more lavish, more extravagant.
I would have it be something you need or want.
But for tonight, it is all that I have to give.
Take it, then, my dear.
Incompleteness is given with all the love I have.

Thursday: Doing love

There's only what you do.
Everything else is inside your head.

But what you do is just the expression
of who you are
and what you know.

And what you do covers a multitude of sins.
You do your tone of voice.
You do the way you cross your legs.
You do the spaces round about you.
You do the silences between your words
as well as the words themselves.
You do the songs you sing.
You do the cup of tea you made your mum.
You do the way you spend your money
and the way you didn't spend it.
You do the love you make
and all the love you didn't make.
You do the atmosphere you change within a room.
You do the rocking of the baby in your arms.

It's what you do that carries me to you and you to me.

But, as already noted, what you do is the expression
of who you are
and what you know.

If who you are feels wrong, or not worth much,
scrunched up in a miserable little ball,
It goes without saying that what you do
will mirror that.
And what others do you will receive
much the same.

And if you think that what you know is useless
or not enough, or not important enough
then what you do will either be under your capacity to do
or will be done more to convince yourself that no one else
has noticed what you don't know.

The thing is
you're all right. Like all the rest.
You'll do just fine.

And what you know, till you know more,
is quite enough
to do love.

Friday: Stations of the cross

Jesus is sentenced to death

The moment you stood out,
the moment you refused any longer to conform,
to fade into the background;
the moment you stopped being nice
and got angry,
confronting us with what we knew about ourselves
but preferred to attribute to others;
the moment we realized that you meant not mastery
but freedom;
in that moment
you signed your own death sentence.

Jesus carries the cross

Your arms are strong.
They have cradled children.
They have broken bread and served it to your friends.
They have prepared a meal for countless empty bellies.
They have stretched to touch and raise and heal.

Your back is strong.
It has carried many cares.
It has bent to stroke a thousand fevered brows
and stooped to wash the dirt from dusty feet.
It has borne the weight of too much expectation.

Strong arms, strong back.
Strong enough for a cross?

Jesus falls for the first time

It's not that you didn't try.
It's not that you wouldn't have carried it
all the way if you could have.
It's just that you had to operate
within the limitations of your strength.
God knows you pushed them back again
and again.
More than you'd thought possible,
more than anyone could have expected.
You tried all right.
But in the end,
it all became too much for you.
It bore you down, and you stumbled, fell.
It's not that you didn't try.

Jesus meets his mother

Oh mother, oh mother.
Here is your hope, your joy, your pride,
staggering up a leprous road to meet you.
Here is your flesh, your blood, your opened womb,
here is your milk, your tears, your sleepless nights.
Here is the ache that rises from between your legs
and splits you upward like a gutting knife.
Here is your skin, the pulse you felt beneath your hand,
here are your eyes, your colour, and the unmistakeable
    smell.
Here are your dreams of feasting at a wedding.
Here is your youthful passion, and your dancing days.
Here is your finest fleshly imprint and your better self.
Here is your child,
staggering up a leprous road to meet you.

Simon of Cyrene carries the cross

You met each other as strangers.
That is to say, you both were strange.
One of you estranged by deed beyond acceptance,
the other picked unerring from the concealing crowd.
But both of you were used to bearing burdens,
had grown accustomed to the lash upon your back.
Was it strange, to know the greatest tenderness that there
    could be
would be to lean upon this strange man's strength?
How often did you ache to lean upon a strong man's
    strength
and find that all your men relied on you?
Strange, that at the end, such tenderness should come
in this strange way, from one a stranger to you.

Veronica wipes the face of Jesus

We know the agony of feeling useless.
We know the scream inside
of absolute and utter powerlessness.
It spawns within us, clawing, gnawing,
and it is fed by what we're forced to watch.
Our eyes grow fat on children's torture;
they swell on every bitter, pointless death.
They bulge with each unnecessary hunger
and vomit out the gross and stupid, stupid waste.
But screams are lost, and self-indulgent.
They do not help the helpless or assuage the bile.
And so we act, even while knowing that our act
is gesture, token, out of all proportion to the pain.
We take the towel; it is the only thing we have.
But still, a gesture, it is something, is it not?
It speaks of more we would do if we could.
It is more than nothing.
Isn't it?

Jesus falls for the second time

Embarrassment, because we know we should help.
Guilt, because we know we could help.
Self-delusion, because we know we would help
if only . . .

Lust, because we secretly enjoy the pleasure.
Anger, because our shame dispels the pleasure.
Nausea, because relief's a sickly pleasure
and yet . . .

Pity, because we are not dead to goodness.
Memory, because we once caught sight of goodness.
Desolation, because this wretchedness suggests the doom
   of goodness
in us . . .

What tangled feelings shimmer on the surface of this
   crowd
as once again, we stand and watch you fall.

Women of Jerusalem weep for Jesus

They are disgusting, your tears.
They are so facile, maudlin, always on display.
You pour them out like water from a jug,
you squander them with little thought for what was paid
to set them flowing.
Save your tears, you daughters of Jerusalem,
and save your easy cheers as well.
Cheers, tears, it's all the same to you.
Emotions lightly conjured up to fit the given mood.
It is enough! Enough of borrowing the deeds of others
to satisfy your own vicarious needs.

Your acts are needed now, there has been too much of
    women weeping.
Dry your tears, resolve instead by your decision
that there will be in future fewer times
for grief like this.
Or, if you will not put your strength and courage
at the service of resistance to the powers,
then weep for your own children, for your daughters'
    daughters.
For, in truth, you will yet live to see them
crushed beneath the weight of mountains, hidden by
    the hills.

Jesus falls for the third time

How can you keep falling?
Why do you not rise?
You don't have to do this
you can lift your eyes.
Look beyond the mountain,
see the other side.
Throw that damned thing over,
why have you no pride?

Why must you keep falling?
Out there, there is space.
You don't have to be here,
you can find your place.
You can still be someone,
leave all this behind.
If you think they'll thank you,
you must have lost your mind.

You could go on falling
from now till kingdom come.
Nobody will bother much,
they'll just think you're dumb.
But they'll be quite happy
to add more to your load.
How much more can you carry?
Do you think you're God?

Please don't go on falling!
It isn't right, you know.
They're getting off too lightly
if you let them use you so.
I don't know what you're doing
or why you're here at all.
I only know that this time
I can't bear to watch you fall.

Jesus is stripped of his robe

The silence is hot.
They're all attentive now.
The sweat is streaming.
The sweat is steaming.
The flush is rising.
The flesh is rising.
The eyes are shifting.
The eyes are drifting.
The heat is sullen.
The threat is sullen.

Gripped, ripped, stripped.
Now you are ready for action.

Jesus is nailed to the cross

Got you!
Now we're going to put you firmly in your place.

Did you really think that we would let you get away
with trying to change what has worked so well
and to the advantage of so many?

A little tinkering here and there—we can allow that.
We are very happy if you want to play with children
or entertain the women (though we would prefer it
if you don't reclaim too many prostitutes).
And healing, well, we all enjoy a happy ending.
Even feeding the poor saves us the bother.

But let me emphasize, there could be no allowance
for the real enormity of what you've done.
You cannot criticize the church.
You cannot undermine the state.
You cannot challenge the establishment
and expect benign approval.

Above all.
Let me hammer home the point . . .
You must not threaten or subvert the patriarchy.
Nor side-step altogether the balance of the powers.
How dare you be so impertinently alive?
That is to threaten God,
and we do not like that. Not at all.

So here you go.
Up against the wall.
Bang! Bang! Bang!

Jesus dies on the cross

Fingered
Taken
Stripped
Spreadeagled
Exposed
Humiliated
Whipped
Mounted
Violated
Broken
Jeered
Handclapped
Spat on
Cursed
Abandoned
Dead

Jesus is taken from the cross (pietà)

She will hold out her arms to you
She will take you upon her knee
She will turn your face to her breast
She will rock you and sing gently to you
She will smooth the hair from your brow
She will wipe the last tear from your brow
She will cover you against the chill air
She will kiss you goodnight.

Children do not die to their mothers
Though the mothers should see them grow cold
Though the knife should betray them
Though the flesh should decay
Though the memory grow old
Though the images fade
Though the pain engulf them.
Children do not die to their mothers.

Ask any mother.

Jesus is laid in the tomb

Will it come to this at last?
Will dreams grow cold? Will freedoms die?
and come to lie in stone?
Will people pause in times to come
and wonder why you tried
to do this new thing, newly;
then shrug, and turn back
to the same old ways?
the same old, sterile ways?
Must flesh and spirit constantly
do battle for a worthless piece of ground,
contest false claims,
arrest each other,
do each other down to death?

Or will the day come ever
when they give up the struggle
and melt, instead, into each other,
and move, and glow, and love each other,
and slip the chastening chain that binds them
dissolve the clay that blinds them?
And flow out of the door of no alternatives
and enter into time and space?

Such power, on such a day, would shatter opposites,
would split the rock, allowing you
to enter and reclaim your darling flesh.
The dead would rise!

But in the absence of surrender, and alternatives,
here is the stone.
Shut the door.
Go away.

Saturday: Send us an angel

*'... send us an angel that will start us seeking a new way
of life ...'*   *(George MacLeod)*

Birth and death come accompanied by angels.
And sometimes, maybe always,
the moment of encounter is the same.

Annunciation — 'you will be changed,
you will give birth to something new.'
And the guardians of the tomb —
'He is not here. Why do you seek the living among the
   dead?'

Lot or Lot's wife-like,
poised between the no-longer and the not-yet,
this I can understand.
This I can, albeit painfully,
give my assent to.

But why did no one warn me
how terrifying angels are?

They are not nice and reassuring,
all dressed in white.
They come with flashing eyes,
and carry flaming swords to pierce your heart.
They come with ruthlessness.

Still, they teach you one thing,
these messengers of God.

I have learned the proper fear of the Lord.

And with this fear, I wait for death, and birth.

Sunday: Resurrection

I do not know
what resurrection is
(though I'm almost sure
it has something to do
with hallowing the common ground).
Of course, that's not all of it.

I expect one day I'll get up
and find that it sneaked up on me
while I wasn't looking,
and maybe even that it's been there all along.
That's as may be.
There's no point in trying to see things
before you're ready.
You have to walk before you can run.

In the meantime,
I believe in it.
And that feels like an initial step.
For now,
it will do.
It is enough.